Chuck and Duck

Written by Sam Hay
Illustrated by Ann Johns

WISE WALRUS

What is synthetic phonics?

Synthetic phonics teaches children to recognise the sounds of letters and to blend 'synthesise' them together to make whole words.

Understanding sound/letter relationships gives children the confidence and ability to read unfamiliar words, without having to rely on memory or guesswork; this helps them progress towards independent reading.

Did you know? Spoken English uses more than 40 speech sounds. Each sound is called a *phoneme*. Some phonemes relate to a single letter (d-o-g) and others to combinations of letters (sh-ar-p). When a phoneme is written down it is called a *grapheme*. Teaching these sounds, matching them to their written form and sounding out words for reading is the basis of synthetic phonics.

Consultant

I love reading phonics has been created in consultation
with language expert Dr Marlynne Grant (Chartered
and Registered Educational Psychologist). For more than
25 years, Marlynne has worked as a regional educational
psychologist, specialising in literacy development for
children of all abilities.

Reading tips

Chuck and Duck focuses on the **ch** sound.

Tricky words in *Chuck and Duck*

Any words in bold do not sound exactly as they look (don't fit the usual sound-letter rules) or are new and have not yet been introduced.

Tricky words in this book:

s**ai**d	t**o**	**f**or	b**a**ll
w**as**	**I**	m**y**	**the**

Extra ways to have fun with *Chuck and Duck*

· After the reader has read the story, ask them questions about what they have just read:

What is Duck good at?
Why did Fred go red?

· Explain that the two letters 'ch' make one sound. Think of other words that use the 'ch' sound, such as chip or chat.

I like to read and quack. My favourite place to read is in the park. Quack!

A pronunciation guide

 This grid contains the sounds used in the story and a guide on how to say them.

s as in sat	a as in ant	t as in tin	p as in pig
i as ink	n as in net	c as in cat	e as in egg
h as in hen	r as in rat	m as in mug	d as in dog
g as in get	o as in ox	u as in up	l as in log
f as in fan	b as in bag	j as in jug	w as in wet
y as in yet	qu as in quiz	ff as in off	ll as in fill
ss as in hiss	ck as in duck	sh as in shop	ch as in chip

Be careful not to add an 'uh' sound to 's', 't', 'p', 'c', 'h', 'r', 'm', 'd', 'g', 'l', 'f' and 'b'. For example, say 'fff' not 'fuh' and 'sss' not 'suh'.

Chuck got a shock.
A duck sat on his mat.

'Yes?' **said** Chuck.
'Quack!' **said** Duck.

Chuck went **to** chop a log.
Duck went as well.

Chuck went **for** a jog.
Duck went as well!

Chuck met his chum Fred,
and his pet dog Chip.

Chuck and Fred had a chat.

'Duck is a dull pet,' **said** Fred.

'Can Duck jump up **for** a **ball**?'
said Fred.

'Not much,' **said** Chuck.

'Can Duck run fast?' **said** Fred.

'Not as such,' **said** Chuck.

'Duck is such a dull pet,' **said** Fred.

Duck went off in a huff.

But Fred and Chuck got a shock.

Duck **was** back.
Duck had set up chess!

A rich man went past.
'**I** wish Duck **was my** pet.
How much?' **said the** man.

'Bad luck,' **said** Chuck.
'Duck is **my** pet and best chum.'
Fred went red!

Other **Level 2** titles to enjoy:

978-1-84898-388-5

978-1-84898-389-2

978-1-84898-386-1

Other titles in the series

Level **1**

978-1-84898-277-2

978-1-84898-396-0

978-1-84898-390-8

978-1-84898-391-5

Level **3**

978-1-84898-397-7

978-1-84898-398-4

978-1-84898-399-1

978-1-84898-400-4

Copyright © Wise Walrus Ltd 2011
First published in Great Britain in 2011 by Wise Walrus
The Pantiles Chambers, 85 High Street, Tunbridge Wells, Kent TN1 1XP
ISBN: 978-1-84898-387-8
Printed in China 10 9 8 7 6 5 4 3 2 1